Cognitive Behavioral Therapy

Master Your Emotions with Over 7 Highly Effective Techniques to Overcome Anxiety, Depression, Anger, and Negative Thoughts - Retrain Your Brain Through CBT Psychotherapy

Stephen Patterson

© Copyright 2019 - All rights reserved.

The content contained within this book may not be reproduced, duplicated or transmitted without direct written permission from the author or the publisher.

Under no circumstances will any blame or legal responsibility be held against the publisher, or author, for any damages, reparation, or monetary loss due to the information contained within this book. Either directly or indirectly.

Legal Notice:
This book is copyright protected. This book is only for personal use. You cannot amend, distribute, sell, use, quote or paraphrase any part, or the content within this book, without the consent of the author or publisher.

Disclaimer Notice:
Please note the information contained within this document is for educational and entertainment purposes only. All effort has been executed to present accurate, up to date, and reliable, complete information. No warranties of any kind are declared or implied. Readers acknowledge that the author is not engaging in the rendering of legal, financial, medical or professional advice. The content within this book has been derived from various sources. Please consult a licensed professional before attempting any techniques outlined in this book.

By reading this document, the reader agrees that under no circumstances is the author responsible for any losses, direct or indirect, which are incurred as a result of the use of information contained within this document, including, but not limited to, — errors, omissions, or inaccuracies.

Contents

Introduction _____ 1

Chapter 1:
CBT Basics _____ 3

Chapter 2:
Basic Exercises _____ 17

Chapter 3:
Dealing with Bad Habits _____ 29

Chapter 4:
Techniques for Dealing with Negative Thoughts _____ 43

Chapter 5:
Techniques for Dealing with Anxiety _____ 63

Chapter 6:
Techniques for Dealing with Fear _____ 81

Chapter 7:
Techniques for Dealing with Depression _____ 93

Chapter 8:
Additional Steps to Take _____ 109

Conclusion _____ 127

COGNITIVE BEHAVIORAL THERAPY

Master Your Emotions with Over 7 Highly Effective Techniques to Overcome Anxiety, Depression, Anger, and Negative Thoughts - Retrain Your Brain Through CBT Psychotherapy

Stephen Patterson

Introduction

The bad news is that more than 60 million adults in America alone are dealing issues related to depression, anger, anxiety, and negative thoughts; the good news is that these issues have been proven to be treatable without the use of medications using cognitive behavioral therapy.

One of the things that sets cognitive behavioral therapy apart from other types of therapy is that you can effectively use it on yourself and the following chapters will discuss the many ways to effectively do just that. First, you will learn all about the basics of cognitive behavioral therapy and what to expect when you are first getting started. Next, things will start out slow with several basic exercises designed to help you relax now. You will then find several exercises dedicated to helping rid you of your bad habits.

From there, you will find specialized exercises devoted to dealing with negative thoughts, anxiety, fear, and depression. Finally, you

Stephen Patterson

will learn about several additional steps you can take to ensure that the time you spend with your chosen cognitive behavioral exercises is as fruitful as possible.

Chapter 1:
CBT Basics

Cognitive behavioral therapy, more commonly known as CBT has a long history of being effective for some people when it comes to dealing with their depression. The core assumption of CBT is that the way that a person feels is directly related to that person's pattern of thoughts. If those thoughts are negative, then they are going to affect that person's mood in a negative way, impacting their sense of self, their behavior, and even their overall physical state. The goal with CBT, then, is to help those with depression learn to recognize their negative thoughts as well as healthy ways of dealing with them.

Additionally, therapists who work with CBT typically strive to help their patients change patterns of behavior that tend to come along with many types of dysfunctional thinking. These patterns often lead to inescapable downward spirals for those with depression which is why changing behavior is so vital to successfully changing mood,

Anxiety and depression are both closely related and are often the result of a misfire or an action that was inappropriate for the situation. For example, someone may experience anxiety because they had a surge of adrenaline driving their vehicle to the store two miles down the road. They would then begin to associate driving with adrenaline. The fight or flight response would kick in each time that they got behind the wheel of a car and they would feel that their life was being threatened.

It could then escalate to an extreme point, and that is the way that anxiety works. It tricks the brain into thinking that normal situations are dangerous. This fight or flight response is a leftover mechanism from the days when humans did need to either run (from a predator) or prepare to fight (that same predator). While most people do not need to run up a tree to get away from a bear or prepare to kill it with their spears, the surge of adrenaline will still come from normal situations, and it is something that people need to overcome.

The same principles work with depression without the Paleolithic feel attached to it. Humans are designed to feel emotions. Sadness is one of the most extreme emotions that a person can feel, and the brain will sometimes get caught in a loop and tell someone to

Cognitive Behavioral Therapy

continuously feel sad. This can be triggered by anything – from a change in physical status to a new job to even...anxiety! The brain will tell the person that he or she needs to become sad for reasons that would normally be considered "every day" and the person would get stuck there. That is the way that depression works in the brain.

Cognitive behavioral therapy works to combat both in the way that it deals with the brain. The point of cognitive behavioral therapy is to trick the brain into getting into a new pattern and retrain it how to think like a "normal" brain. CBT is as simple as a training method that will teach a person by retraining their brain to think in a way that makes sense.

Task based: What really sets CBT apart from other types of therapies is the fact that it is structured around completing a pair of different tasks. Cognitive restructuring (discussed in detail in the next chapter) and behavioral activation (the chapter after that). CBT also places most of its focus on the present, emphasizing the way the patient feels in the moment more than the underlying reasons a person might feel a specific way.

Focused on the now: CBT is also known to focus on specific problems the patient might be facing as opposed to the more general picture or their overall mental state. In either group, or individual sessions, problem thinking, and behavior will be first identified, then prioritized and finally addressed in order of necessity. This makes CBT inherently goal oriented with patients and therapists working together in order to meet specific goals, both during sessions and for the week in general.

Promotes education: CBT is primarily education based which means that the therapist is going to use structured learning experiences as a way for patients to learn to monitor the negative thoughts and images that come into their minds. The goal, then, is to recognize how these negative ideas affect the physical condition and behavior and to understand how these things affect mood.

How It Works

The success of CBT relies heavily on the strength of the relationship the patient has with their therapist. The best therapists do not expect the patient to depend on them to pull them out of their current state but works to empower them by teaching specific strategies they can use to pull themselves out.

Cognitive Behavioral Therapy

In the early sessions, therapists will focus on understanding how the patient perceives the world around them, so they can create methods that can help them make changes. This is done by applying these basic principles:

There Is A Time Limit

Unlike other forms of therapy where the sessions could last for months or even years, CBT sessions generally run for about 10 to 15 weekly sessions on average. This time limit has several benefits. First, it cuts back on the costs for the patient, but it also motivates them to work harder. There is no sense in putting it off for another week because at some point the sessions will come to an end.

It Must be Based on Evidence

The techniques used in CBT are backed by extensive research and proven studies. Decisions on treatment are not based on guesswork or opinions but instead are based on the experiences of thousands of others that have gone through it before. Even the estimation of how long a treatment should last needs to be based on empirical evidence.

Each Session Is Focused on The Patient's Goals

Goals are not given arbitrarily, but the patient sets their own goals that they want to address in the here and now. The patient is also given the chance to gauge whether the therapy is helping them meet their goals or not.

The Entire Process Is Collaborative

This means that responsibility for fixing the behavior does not lie entirely on the therapist, but it is a combined effort designed to meet the patient's unique set of needs.

Stages Of CBT

The goal of CBT isn't to listen to each and every issue that you have going on in your life in an effort to diagnose you with a fancy sounding illness, it is to get to the root of the biggest problems in your life and find ways to make it easier for you to deal with them on a daily basis. The goal, then can either be to change the way you think or determine where specific maladaptive behaviors are located and work to squash them specifically.

The best way to go about doing so is using a cognitive behavioral assessment which is made up of five key steps. First, you are going to want to determine the primary behaviors that are in play. Next, you are going to want to determine if the behaviors in question are either good or bad before then looking at the negative behaviors that you have uncovered in order to determine their frequency, duration, and intensity. From there you will want to determine the most beneficial course of action you can embark on in order to correct any relevant negative behaviors. Finally, you will want to determine how effective the treatment is and make changes accordingly.

Therapeutic alliance: This process is going to be overseen by a therapist, which means the first step to completing CBT successfully is find a therapist that you can form what is known as a therapeutic alliance with. This alliance is built on a relationship of mutual trust and respect, that can then be leveraged to generate solutions for the problems that are created as a result. This doesn't happen immediately, of course, and instead, every CBT experiences starts with a session where you and the therapist get to know one another in an effort to decide if the relationship is going to be a good fit for everyone to ensure that you get what you need from the process.

Strive to control your thoughts: After you manage to successfully form a therapeutic alliance, you will be ready to really get into the meat and potatoes of CBT. You and your therapist will begin by discussing your most relevant problems, as well as how to start dealing with them successfully, often by controlling your thought processes in one way or another. This, in turn, often requires that you come to an understanding regarding why you think the way you do. To get at this truth, you and your therapist will discuss your past as well as how it connects to where you currently find yourself in life.

You will find that many of your thought patterns often stem from a specific issue that occurred in your past which has altered the way you think in one way or another. These are referred to as schemas and you will find that if you can isolate the negative ones you can move forward successfully.

Additionally, you are going to need to take a closer look at the preconceptions that you are dealing with as a means of determining why they might exist in the first place. During this period, you will often receive homework from your therapist that will include exercises to practice regularly that will help you change out your negative thoughts and replace them with new positive habits instead. There is no time strict time limit for this stage as it will vary based on the issues you are currently dealing with. However, a guided CBT session rarely lasts more than 16 weeks though most patients begin to see results almost immediately, assuming they do their homework that is.

Generate new patterns: Once you start to regain full control of your thoughts, your therapist will then begin to suggest new ways you can develop productive thought patterns as a means of replacing the negative ones that have been removed from your life. This stage of your CBT experience focuses primarily on practicing these new patterns until they become second nature.

During this time, you and your therapist will also brainstorm additional exercises in hopes of helping you to strengthen the positive patterns you are trying to create. In much the same way the previous step focused on regaining control of your thoughts, this step is about regaining control of your actions. You will know that you are ready to move on to the final stage after you begin using the techniques you have learned without thinking twice about it.

Moving forward: The last phase of any CBT experience starts when you successfully feel as though you can handle your issues and any new ones that may arise on your own with the help of your therapist coaching you through the specifics. This step is not about leaving your CBT exercises behind; however, it just means you will be in full control of your treatment and responsible for giving yourself the structure you need to keep up with your new habits.

One of the most important aspects of CBT, and one that sets it apart from other types of therapy is that it is entirely possible to practice CBT all by yourself, as long as you are very careful to ensure you are only promoting the right types of behaviors from the jump. This is what the rest of the book will be focused on providing you, a structure by which you can get started with CBT by yourself.

CBT can be used successfully in a wide variety of ways for self-instruction including things like creating new coping strategies, setting goals and improving relaxation techniques. It has also proven just as effective in one-on-one settings as it is in group sessions. The one thing CBT isn't great for is short-term only work as it is rare that after 16 weeks the issues patients are dealing with are done completely, follow-up personal maintenance work is almost always required.

Maximize your CBT experience
In order to maximize the time, you spend practicing CBT exercises, there are numerous things you can do right from the start to improve your effectiveness.

Understand what you are signing up for: While meeting potential therapists in person is an important part of the full CBT experience, there are still things you can do in order to ensure you hit it off with the therapists you do meet in person. After working through the exercises in this book you will have a fairly good idea of what works for you which means you can simply focus on someone that prefers the same types of exercises you do. Narrowing down your list of potential therapists from the start is much faster than learning the details about each of them once you are in the office and potentially even paying by the hour.

You should also always take the time to look at reviews from other patients to see what types of cases they tend to treat most frequently. If you find yourself having trouble finding something that seems like a good fit, start by asking your friends and family, you never know who is going to turn out to be practicing CBT as well.

Mentally prepare before you start: Even if you are, broadly speaking, open to the idea of CBT from the start, change of the magnitude that it often posits can be difficult to fully get behind. Doing what you can to ensure you are mentally onboard for the process will make it easier for you to undertake the practice with the focus and the drive that it requires in order to truly move forward successfully. As such, you will want to leave your comfort zone behind you and never look back which means you need to jump into the practice firmly with both feet. Only by committing to the practice wholeheartedly will you see the ultimate results.

Likewise, there are plenty of different types of exercises discussed in the following chapters and, even if they don't necessarily pertain to your specific issue on the surface, it is important to try them out before moving forward. Only by trying everything out will you be able to authoritatively say if they work for you or not. After all, there is no reason to rush through the various exercises discussed within, they aren't going anywhere and you never know what benefits you might see simply by giving them a try and taking the time to let their potential benefits manifest themselves once and for all.

Finally, if you have been toying with the idea of giving CBT a try you may instead find that fully giving yourself over to the process is far more likely to yield real success. In fact, studies show that fully committing improves your chance of long-term success by more than 50 percent. This isn't to say that you need to continue with CBT forever, and eventually you will want to set an end date for your practice to ensure you can truly make the changes you may otherwise continue to put off indefinitely. Spend some time and think about the context of your plan before considering when setting a firm timetable will be right for you.

Stephen Patterson

Chapter 2:
Basic Exercises

When stress floods the body in large quantities over a short period of time it triggers the body's flight or fight response. While you certainly won't be able to avoid every flight or fight response that gets in your way, by taking the time to learn how to enter a relaxation response at will, you should find that you are able to control your emotional outbursts far more reliably than may otherwise be the case. The relaxation state essentially puts the brakes on the flight or fight response, and thus anything that happens as a response to it and forces your mind back into a state of complete equilibrium.

This isn't just a mental response either, having a true relaxation response will increase the flow of blood to the brain, cause your muscles to relax, stabilize your blood pressure, normalize your heart rate and slow your breathing. Beyond these measurable physical effects, this exercise will also temporarily boost productivity and motivation, enhance your problem-solving abilities and even temporarily improve focus and increase energy.

What's more, there is no one right way to achieve a true relaxation response, which means there is a perfect way to practice entering this state out there for everyone. The one caveat to this is that passive activities like reading a book or watching television, while certainly relaxing, aren't enough to generate the physical effects of a true relaxation response. The right relaxation technique is going to be one that focuses your mind and interrupts your regular stream of thoughts enough to elicit the type of physical response you should be aiming for. The exercises discussed in this chapter are designed to help you reach this state or to make the state easier to reach in general

Proper breathing techniques: CBT teaches that thoughts, behaviors, and feelings all come together to affect your physical well-being. With that in mind, it then makes sense to think that treating any type of anxiety, depression or phobia-based fear would require physical, as well as mental, action. For an example, simply think back to the last time you had an overwhelming attack of your symptoms and consider how it changed the way you felt physically and how quickly the change occurred.

In many instances, when things become too overwhelming the first thing that begins to suffer is your breathing. The way you breathe directly impacts everything else relating to the way your body functions. If you are receiving either too little or too much oxygen it can significantly enhance the seriousness of other symptoms causing a mild attack to quickly snowball into a serious incident.

The good news is that learning to control your breathing is quite simple once you start consciously thinking about it. The easiest means of doing so is through the 4-7-8 method. To practice this method, all you need to do is find a comfortable place to sit, sit up straight and breathe in slowly for four seconds. You will then hold your breath for seven seconds and then breathe out slowly for a total of eight seconds. You will want to repeat this process for about two minutes, or six repetitions. You may find it helpful to close your eyes during this process, though it is purely up to personal preference.

While you might not notice anything at first, with practice you will find that everything around you starts to slow down, and as your heartbeat follows suit you should become more relaxed. If you don't seem to see much benefit from a two-minute session, try extending it out to five or even 10, it's all about finding the right amount of time to counteract the other physical effects your body is currently experiencing.

Progressive muscle relaxation: progressive muscle relaxation is a technique, like measured breathing, that can be used in the moment to deal with particularly bad anxiety flair ups. It involves tensing and then relaxing specific groups of muscles as a means of distracting your anxiety and short circuiting the loop that causes it to manifest in the first place. This is since it is difficult for your body to maintain a tensed, anxious state, and a relaxed calm state at the same time. As such, if you feel an anxiety attack coming your way, a period of focused relaxation may be just what you need to cut it off at the pass. You may also find this type of exercise useful if you are having difficulty sleeping.

While you will eventually be able to use this exercise in the moment, while you are still getting the hang of it you are going to want to find some place quiet where you can focus on the task at hand. Give yourself 15 to 20 minutes of practice time to start, though once you get the hang of it you will likely be able to experience the same results in far less time. To start, you simply need to pick a specific part of your body and shift the entirety of your focus to it. This step will be the same regardless of which muscle group you are focusing on.

Cognitive Behavioral Therapy

For example, if you wanted to start with your left hand, you would hold it out in front of you, so you can focus on it fully. Then, while breathing slowly, in and out, you are going to want to tense all the muscles in your hand as hard as possible, for between five and ten seconds. You should tense hard enough that the tension starts to feel uncomfortable by the point time is up, though you should obviously refrain from tensing so hard that you hurt yourself. The goal here is to fully focus all the tension you are feeling in general into the tension you feel in your hand.

Journaling: your thoughts are a continuous stream; there is no waking moment where you aren't thinking about something. It may not also be in the front of your mind, but thoughts are always present and always moving. As the adage goes, "I think, therefore I am." It's difficult to recognize everything that passes through our heads as it is. Throw anxiety into the mix and it becomes impossible to follow everything.

A journal is a great way to track your anxiety. By putting your thoughts on paper you'll give them tangible form. Though like a diary, an anxiety journal isn't for just a record of your daily happenings. It's closer to an operating table where you'll examine, dissect, and explore your distressing thoughts. This is helpful in several ways:

Better self-expression: how often have you tried to explain your anxiety to someone only to feel like they didn't fully understand what you were saying? It's difficult to articulate worry, especially now. But no one will have a better understanding of your thought processes than you do. By laying it out on the page you can practice how you can communicate it to others. In therapy sessions, you can even read your entries to your therapist.

Self-reflection: as we become more aware of ourselves and our thought cycles it can become easy to let thoughts get lost in the blur. If you have a written record of your thoughts it acts likes a map of sorts. You can see what sort of thoughts you had on any given day and see how they changed overtime, creating pathways and patterns that you can recognize overtime. This recognition will help you develop plans going forward.

Progress: it's also beneficial to have the journal of your thoughts because it shows how much progress you make on your journey to recovery. But of equal value to these positives is seeing where you come short. If you're honest in writing all the highs and lows, you'll have examples of moments that need improvement.

You are going to want to make a point of only writing down your emotions at the end of each day as this will give you time to really reflect on each of the instances in question as opposed to writing them down so that they paint a specific picture or only show that you are making progress in a specific direction. Once you have a decent cross section of experiences that you have regularly you can begin to take note of similarities and difference in specific scenarios that may have ultimately led to different emotional responses or reactions to a response. Forewarned is forearmed and understanding how certain situations influence your future emotions will make it easier to start to manage them successfully.

ACCEPTS: another useful set of actions has been developed as a method of distraction. These are used so that when a distasteful emotion or situation comes up, you can start to distract yourself and divert your attention away from it in a productive manner. This will aid you in helping you to deal with the emotional response. This also goes hand in hand with your mindfulness practice (discussed in a later chapter) because the focusing ability that you develop when working with mindfulness will allow you to quickly draw your attention elsewhere and handle the things that are happening inside your head.

You can remember these actions through the acronym *ACCEPTS*. The letters in the acronym spell out a few different key ideas.

The first key idea is activities: when you need to distract yourself from something which is happening, try to divert your attention towards something else that you enjoy. This will take up your energy for a productive and positive emotional experience rather than one which will cause you to feel negatively and potentially even helpless.

The next key idea is contribution: instead of focusing on yourself and the things happening to you in your immediate vicinity, focus instead on how you can help others or the people around you. Use your time and resources and skills in order to make people around you feel better. This also has the additional benefit that it will make you feel like you're a better and more productive person than you did before, which will raise your level of productivity and your general feeling of self-worth. This has a reflexive benefit in that it starts to make you value yourself and feel slightly better.

The next key idea that you need to focus on building in the ACCEPTS distraction method is comparisons: Really, this idea is all about your perspective. Compare yourself both to how others are feeling in addition to the progress that you've made so far.

While it is possible that you are not in all that great of a position now, it is important to keep in mind that there is always someone out there who is worse off than you are. Remember, that no matter how bad things are you are not at rock bottom yet and start from there. Regardless of your current state you can take a mental inventory and compare where you are now to where you started out. CBT is all about making slow and steady progress with the goal of building new and improved habits over time. Keeping tabs on the progress that you have made is not only a great way to ensure you are on the right track, but it can also help get you back there if you have temporarily strayed.

This is where emotions come in as you are going to need to help ensure you are feeling different emotions than those you feel in the moment. Thinking about something that makes you laugh or feel happy is a great place to start, as is focusing on a hobby you have that you know will help to alter your headspace for good. Anything you can do to make yourself feel different is the right choice as this will give you the time you need to put yourself into a more useful headspace.

From there, you are going to want to practice pushing the negative emotion away. The goal here is to be able to put the current situation out of your mind for long enough that you can change your mind set for good. This will go hand in hand with the practice of mindfulness that is discussed in a later chapter. Being able to mentally push things away from your perspective is a core facet of mindfulness and it will also help you to control your mindset regardless of the situation you may find yourself in. While this doesn't mean you have to like whatever situation you find yourself in, you will find that pushing the thought out of your mind is a great way to calm yourself down now.

You will be using this practice to force yourself to think about something else. Use the steps outlined above to clear off your mental highway so that you can escape the traffic jam of your negative thoughts and emotions and start fresh once more. This will come in handy when it comes to dealing with sensations which are essentially visceral reactions that you can't exactly resist. Sudden shocks to your system are a great way to break your mind out of its current state and have it focus on something else for long enough that things reset, and you are able to continue in a more restrained fashion. The logic here is the same as if you pinch yourself to distract from a stubbed toe, your body can only focus on one sensation at a time so by choosing the sensation to choose you to take back control.

Those ideas outline the central basis of the accepts distraction strategy. A bright idea would be to put them all on note cards and summarize them, then refresh yourself every morning when you wake up and every night before you go to bed when you're doing your distress tolerance block. These will help you in developing tolerance skills for distasteful or stressful situations.

Stephen Patterson

Chapter 3:
Dealing with Bad Habits

The time it takes to form a behavioral habit is not a precise science. There are so many factors at play that serve as variables. It's better to think of it this way: it happens when it happens. You must work towards it, of course, but it's ultimately a long-term goal. Even if you feel like you've achieved your goal you should still act as though you are working toward it. Don't put a time limit on your personal growth!

In a nutshell, the formation of good habits is based on two ideas: your long-term goal—that is, the habit you are working to develop—and a series of smaller achievements you use as guideposts to motivate you. The smaller goals are really steppingstones, and to be honest most people who give up on the development of better habits fall short because they set their final goal and aim for it right away without any sort of practice or buildup.

Let's use an example everyone can understand. We all want to exercise more, right? But lots of us jump into it right away with only the end goal in mind and get discouraged when things turn out to be more difficult than they had first expected. Let's say that you want to start running a mile a day, and you haven't been running regularly for a while, if ever. In this instance, you aren't conditioned for it and shooting for that one-mile goal will be an uphill battle.

That's why it's beneficial to break it down into smaller pieces. Depending on your fitness level you may start by running a quarter mile every other day to ease yourself into it. Once you've done this for a while it feels easy for you, try running a quarter mile every day. When that challenge is conquered add more distance. Keep adding until you've reached your goal of one mile every day.

ACT

First pioneered in the 1980s, acceptance and commitment therapy, more commonly known as ACT, is a variation of CBT that promotes growth through the exploration of new behaviors rather than seeking to remove negative feelings directly. This is done with the help of many behavior altering strategies that are then designed to increase mental flexibility which makes it easier to commit to the process in both the short and the long run. Essentially, ACT is a process of learning to be more aware of your negative impulses and thoughts through the act of practicing to ignore them in such a way that they do not impact your day-to-day life.

The main goal of ACT is to learn the most effective way possible when it comes to controlling your thoughts, feelings, sensations, and memories by sorting the negative from the positive without interacting with the negative thoughts directly, much like you would do while practicing mindfulness meditation. In fact, ACT uses many variations of mindfulness practices to help practitioners remain in the moment as much as possible.

Another interesting fat about ACT is that it works based on the assumption that all humans have destructive thoughts and, as such, those with mental illnesses are in no way less "normal" than anyone else, their thoughts just come on stronger sometimes than they might like. ACT traces the root of all psychological issues to a combination of the unduly rigid psyche, unnecessary cognitive entanglement or extreme feelings of avoidance. This combination, in turn, serves to prevent those who are burdened with it from cultivating the types of patterns and actions that make it possible to achieve your desired goals.

The acronym FEAR is used to outline what ACT perceives to be the root of most mental issues:

- **F**use thoughts and actions

- **E**xpand on experiences

- **A**void what your senses are telling you

- **R**eframe the situation to promote negative patterns

Perhaps unsurprisingly the opposite of FEAR is ACT:

- **A**ccept the truth and try and keep your focus on the present

- **C**reate a plan and stick with it

- **T**ime to act on your plan

Primary Focus

In addition to its two acronyms, ACT focuses on six discreet steps with the goal of allowing those who always practice it to be more mentally flexible.

Escape negative thoughts: The first step in ACT is to understand that you tend to focus on the negative and work to minimize this tendency as much as possible. This can be done through a personal vigilance that ensures you stop yourself from returning to negative images, emotions, memories or thoughts even though there is really nothing to be gained from doing so.

If you find the allure of these negative thoughts too powerful to overcome, then you might find that taking advantage of the mind palace technique is an especially effective way to ensure this part of the process goes off without a hitch. The mind palace technique works by making it easy for you to construct a place for your thoughts to live both so that you can remember them and also so you can control them and ensure they don't pop out when they are uninvited.

To start you need to visualize a physical space with which you are exceedingly familiar. Contrary to the name, the space can either be large or small, what matters is that you can think about the space and visualize yourself there completely. You need to be able to picture the way the space feels, sounds, smells and you need to be able to move between the rooms effortlessly as if you were walking them in person. Once you have visualized the space you will need to do everything in your power to carve out a space for it in your mind, really ground it in place so that it will always look the same when you come back to it. There is no need to rush this part of the process if you need to spend several days getting the memory just right then do so.

Next, you will need to go about populating all the rooms with your memories and grouping them together in ways that will make it easy for you to peruse them later and look at everything stored within. For example, if your mind palace is your childhood home, then you could store all the recipes you know in a recipe book in the kitchen along with the memories of all the good meals you have even eaten. Again, the size of the space isn't important in this scenario and if your space is small you can visualize shelves where you keep various memories in snow globes. The specifics don't matter if the storage system works for you and it allows you to easily recall the memories stored in each space.

You are going to want to store the bad memories with the good as it is only by experiencing the bad in the world that we can fully appreciate the good. With, some memories are going to be so hurtful and unruly that the only real solution is to lock them up and throw away the key. To deal with these types of memories appropriate you simply need to visualize a deep dark place for them to go, lock them up and throw away the key. This should then make it far easier for you to prevent them from showing up on their own.

Look inward: Without having to worry about negative thoughts popping up uninvited you should find that it is ultimately much easier to look at yourself with a critical eye, making it easier for you to find the most reasonable path to your goals. It is also important to understand the difference between the reality of the situation that you are presented with as opposed to the way your cognitive distortions are making things look now. If you take the time required to really poke and prod the differences you should be able to determine when your mind is simply creating unnecessary static that is making it more difficult to see clearly and when your path is being blocked by more serious issues.

Find the patterns: After you are truly aware of your goals and how to best to go about reaching them, it will become even easier for you to find the patterns that are keeping you from achieving them. Viewing these patterns will, in turn, make it easier for you to determine your true values and what matters to you most. Understanding your values will make it easier for you to ensure they are a part of all you do. While it is important to determine what your common patterns of behavior are, it is equally important not to overdo it.

The human brain likes patterns, so much so that it will even create them where they don't exist if you look hard enough. In your quest to better understand yourself, it is important to not commit yourself to avoiding patterns that do not actually exist.

FAT

Functional analytic therapy, commonly abbreviated as FAT, is another commonly used variation of traditional CBT practices which places more of a focus on the therapeutic alliance in hopes of using this connection as a catalyst for positive change in the patient's life. This type of practice allows the therapist to more directly work the patient through a program known as contingent responding where they bring up positive, specific behaviors and responses that the patient has had and encourage them to continue while simultaneously downplaying other, similar, negative responses or coping mechanisms that may still be in play.

A key facet of this variation of CBT is active listening on the part of the therapist who will use it as a means of reinforcing the positive behaviors even more. This approach should ultimately lead the patient to feel more in control of their actions which should naturally lead them to more personal breakthroughs as a result. The belief at the heart of FAT is that when an outside party can point out the

Cognitive Behavioral Therapy

negative behaviors that a person might not see, it then becomes much easier for the person to take positive actions moving forward. Additionally, the reason that many people find changing existing habits to be so difficult is that any regret they might feel about not changing the habit only occurs well after it is too late to do anything about it.

In this scenario, it may help to picture your subconscious mind as an untrained puppy which means that it will require plenty of immediate and direct feedback in order to ensure that positive change happens the first time and then continues to happen regularly thereafter. Therefore, it is important to use a therapist for FAT to be effective as the suggestions that come from a position of authority will naturally bypass the filters that you may otherwise have in place that ensure the status quo is maintained.

This is why it is so important for the patient/therapist relationship to be nurtured in the right way as doing so will ensure that the patient is able to experience various emotions and thoughts that are associated with their issues during treatment sessions as clearly as they would out in the real world. Patients will also be taught a wide variety of behaviors they are sure to find useful when it comes to creating behaviors that are focused and based on results, regardless of how well the actual action ends up being performed as a means of teaching their minds that more positive reinforcement is never far away.

Set the Right Goals

Be Accountable: The concept of being accountable is highly important and powerful in the realm of willpower. The notion behind this is that being left to your personal choices makes it far too easy to make rationalizations and excuses to avoid something. This could be feeling tired, overworked, or any other various state. Our minds don't tend to care too much about how valid an excuse is, if it can find one to use. This is because our minds crave familiarity and resist that which is new. Thankfully, a solution exists, and it isn't even complicated or hard.

This solution is creating structures that will keep you living up to a better standard and not making up petty excuses or rationalizations for not achieving your goals. Plenty of possibilities exist for this, such as getting an exercise partner or personal coach. Whichever system you decide to implement, what matters is that you are diminishing the likelihood that you will make up excuses and procrastinate, and will instead stay with your goals and real, personal values in life.

Getting rid of distraction: Every human being is susceptible to distraction and temptation, it's part of who we are. Our modern world makes this even more difficult given the sheer number of available distractions on the internet. Realizing all of this, it's crucial that we come up with a plan for protecting our productivity from these temptations.

Now, none of the above distractions are inherently bad, but they sure can hold us back when we should instead be using our energy for achieving our goals. How should we work with this? The first step is to identify your temptations and distractions, such as Twitter or YouTube. Next, come up with a method for preventing them from stealing your attention away.

Be Smart about your Goals: Achieving your dreams isn't only about setting quality goals, but about being smart about them. This means getting very clear cut, detailed, and as specific as possible. Why is having specific goals so important? They give your life a direction and purpose, allowing you to see the connection between how you live from moment to moment, and how your life looks overall. Your goals should all meet the criteria of being timely, relevant to your life, achievable, measurable, and as detailed and specific as possible.

Specific: A goal that is specific has distinct and separate states of success and failure which means it is already statistically more likely to be accomplished than a goal that is extremely vague. When it comes to choosing appropriately specific goals, consider who you can turn to for help in completing the goal, the target for the goal in question, where you will need to be to attain the goal as well as when you want the goal to be completed. Finally, you will need to consider any potential restraints that will keep you from success. You will know you have the right goal in mind when you have the answer to all 6 specifics.

Measurable: SMART goals are measurable. When it comes to choosing the goals that you are going to set for yourself, it is important that what you choose has a degree of success that is associated with it. Only by understanding when you have done poorly will you even be able to realistically hope to improve. There are many scenarios that can arise that will find you feeling as though you are making progress when in reality you are doing little more than spinning your wheels and setting measurable goals will help prevent you from finding yourself in this scenario.

The best way to keep your goals measurable is to set up a generalized timetable based on whatever it is that you have planned for yourself and then keep track of how you are doing in relation to it. This timetable won't need to be extremely precise, if it has specific deadlines that you can always actively be working towards than it is doing its job. Keeping tabs on your success in chunks will ensure that you not only start off on the right foot but keep that success up all the way through to the finish line as well.

Attainable: SMART Goals are always attainable. Ideal scenarios are nice but including goals that have only a slim probability of materializing is doing little more than wasting your team's time. This is not saying that complicated or difficult goals should be avoided, rather it is about realistically knowing your limits and when they can be expanded. Setting long-term goals is good for the self-image of the business and it can help every member of the team grow to reach them.

Realistic: A realistic goal is one that your team is both able and willing to strive for in the current climate. It doesn't matter if you would be able to accomplish the goal if another set of circumstances were true, focus on the here and now and work from there. Realistic goals are also those that are set at a level where it will require work to reach them while at the same time not requiring too much work that they seem forever out of reach. Realistic goals that require a moderate amount of effort from the team to achieve tend to create the most motivational force.

Timely: A good goal is one that as a clear timetable for when it is going to be completed. Even the best-intentioned goals are likely to fall apart if their timetable is to strict, but also if it is too generous. Timetables that are too condensed increase the odds of requiring you too cut corners in order to find success while those that are too long can be beset by unexpected complications that would have been avoided had the timetable been a little shorter. Finding the right timeframe is key to keeping your motivation levels at the right point to ensure success in a reasonable period.

Chapter 4:
Techniques for Dealing with Negative Thoughts

CBT is based on the premise that it isn't the situation or circumstances that cause the condition, but the meaning assigned to these situations that lead to us experience depression or anxiety. The way we interpret a situation is what makes us slip into a negative state of mind. Often, the ideas that we hold about events or situations are impractical or blown out of proportion.

When these misleading notions are not challenged, they continue to grow stronger and lead to even more negativity. We assume it as our reality, which blocks us from perceiving things as they are and leading a fulfilling life. There is a tendency to overlook or ignore things that do not match our negative perception of events and situations. We continue to let these thoughts grow unhindered.

For instance, a person suffering from depression will think that he/she just can't go to the office today because nothing's going to be positive. Their thoughts operate from a sense of hopelessness.

They end up believing what they think is true. So according to the person, nothing positive is bound to happen at work today, which means with their negative thought pattern there's absolutely no opportunity of knowing if this feeling is right or wrong. The person doesn't give himself/herself a chance to ascertain the veracity of their claims. Their thinking itself leads to a negative or unpleasant experience.

In the above example, the person stays at home and doesn't go to work. Thus he/she doesn't know whether their negative prediction had any clear basis. He/she sits at home thinking that they are an absolute failure and that they've let people down. They become angry with themselves and think about how incompetent and useless they are. This leads to the person feeling even worse than earlier, which results in more difficulty while attending office the following day. This causes a downward thinking, behaving and feeling spiral or a vicious circle that leads to several problems.

Emotional resistance: As you first start shifting your mindset, you might find some emotional resistance within yourself against making the switch. This could be confusing—after all, why would anyone want to stay in a negative frame of mind?

Cognitive Behavioral Therapy

We often adopt negative mindsets as a defense mechanism, in order to protect ourselves from suffering. This seems counter-intuitive since we are suffering when we are feeling negative all the time. However, when we are negative, we set our expectations low, often giving into doubt and pessimism to prevent ourselves from getting our hopes up. If we never get our hopes up, then we can't be disappointed when things don't work out. As sad as it is, many people find it easier to cope with being negative all the time rather than dealing with intense moments of disappointment and failure. What these people don't realize is that those feelings are only temporary and that they bring opportunities for learning and growth. They are living with a fixed mindset, in which failure is absolute.

The truth of the matter is there are two main ways of perceiving personal ability and one or the other was likely imparted unto you as a small child, without either you or the person doing the imparting truly understanding the magnitude of what had occurred. One mindset sees ability, intelligence and internal motivation as characteristics that one is born with, while the other sees them for what they truly are, goals that can be achieved with hard work and dedication. This second mindset is referred to as a growth mindset and it should be obvious which of the two you are going to want to cultivate if you want to ever have a shot at empowering yourself in the long term.

Growth-Oriented Mindset

- Appreciates constructive criticism

- Inspired by the success of others

- Treats obstacles as tools for learning

- Appreciates challenge

- Understands that effort and success are linked

- Focused on the long term

Fixed Mindset

- Does not listen to feedback

- Finds the success of others threatening

- Believes effort and success are not linked

- Gives up when presented with roadblocks

- Prefers to avoid challenging situations

- Prioritizes looking competent over subtle skill

Changing your mindset is all about committing to the task at hand and changing small thoughts regarding your ability to change in general. Over time, you will be able to consciously alter larger thoughts which will then make it easier to take more active control over your mindset.

When working to keep a growth mindset in all things, it is important to keep it up even when the going gets tough. It will likely seem like the easiest thing in the world to do while things are going well, but a fixed mindset is much more likely to manifest itself during times when roadblocks begin presenting themselves. Your fixed mindset will likely make you want to abandon all hope of forward progress when these roadblocks appear.

If you feel emotional resistance to shifting toward a positive mindset, ask yourself why. Likely, when you dig deep enough, you will find that on some level there is a part of you that is afraid of getting hurt. Realize that life is full of ups and downs, and that you can choose to be negative all the time, or you can choose to be positive and handle the tough moments in life as they come, one at a time. With a positive mindset, you will find that you have the strength to overcome the hardest trials, and the more effort you put into your positive thinking, the less power that fear will hold over you as time goes on.

Cognitive distortion: A cognitive distortion is a biased perspective that a person takes on about themselves or the world around them. At their heart, they are always irrational thoughts that are reinforced, either knowingly or unknowingly over time. These patterns and systems of thoughts are often extremely subtle, so much so, that it can be difficult to recognize them because they are such a common part of your daily thoughts. This is exactly what makes them so potentially dangerous as it is exceedingly difficult to change things that you can't perceive need to be changed.

While cognitive distortions come in many different forms, they are all going to have some things in common, starting with the fact that they are all patterns or tendencies in belief or thought. They are also always going to contain the potential to cause psychological damage in addition to being patently inaccurate and false.

When first taking stock of your cognitive distortions, you may find it difficult or frightening that there is something out there that is influencing your thoughts without your conscious say in the matter.

It is important to keep it up, however, as the only way you can ever hope to overcome your distortions is to shine the brightest light you possibly can on them. It is also important to keep in mind that dealing with multiple cognitive distortions at once is an exceedingly common incident. If you are human, you are going to experience them, it is as simple as that.

Triggers: Every person has a trigger, something that will set them off and often results in their emotions taking the reins and causing a lot of issues. They may have been fine doing stuff and then that trigger will push them to be angry, mad, upset or something else. Often those emotions take over control so much that they will end up doing things that they regret later. One of the biggest things that you need to do when working on your emotional intelligence is learning how to recognize these triggers so that you can avoid them and keep your emotions under control.

Everyone has a trigger when it comes to their emotions. It is not random when you get mad and explode at the people around you. If you want to start working on your emotional intelligence and get it to work for you, it is important that you learn what some of these triggers are all about.

For many people, the triggers that come with anger would include something that stress or insecurities. When they are dealing with a lot of stress at work or home or elsewhere, they are more likely to lash out at even the smallest thing. But is it worth harming other people and making them feel bad because you are a little bit stressed out about something? Learning how to properly manage your stress levels and keep them low is one of the best things that you can do in this situation.

Removing triggers: Once you have managed to make a list of your triggers, the next thing you are going to want to do is everything in your power to ensure you remove them from your general line of sight until you have your new habits down pat. While you will rarely be able to remove absolutely all the power a given trigger has, you should be able to lessen it significantly, with practice. It is important to keep in mind that the early days are likely going to be tough going, but each time you withstand a serious temptation it will get a little easier.

Build a routine: Regardless of your goals, if you aren't already maintaining a schedule where you can eat regularly, then it is important to make doing so a priority. Not only will eating at regular periods help you to feel better, but it will also ensure that your brain has the fuel required to make good decisions. Specifically, studies show that those with low blood sugar are three times more likely to make poor decisions based on a lack of resolve than those whose blood sugar was on point. Don't let something as simple as a lack of food trigger a relapse into behavior you are trying to avoid. Rather, make it a point of keeping healthy snacks on hand to ensure that you are always able to keep a clear head no matter what.

Disarming negative thought traps: If your anxious thoughts include a fear of never being better at a crucial activity or skill, then you should replace those thoughts with something more positive such as:

- I have made changes before and can do so again.
- I have a support system in place that will help me through this difficult time.
- I must simply take things one day at a time.
- Don't beat yourself up, at least you are trying.

If you have anxiety surrounding food or the amount of food, you eat in relation to the amount of weight you may gain then you could replace the thought with something more productive in the vein of:

- No one food has that amount of power over me.
- There are plenty of healthy reasons to eat this item of food.
- A vast majority of foods are fine in moderation.
- One of these is not going to make me gain weight.
- Additional coping statements you may find useful include:
- Just go for it.
- Taking time for myself is perfectly acceptable.
- My anxiety does not define me.
- Food is fuel.
- I am smart, health and strong.
- I can make good choices.
- My life is mine to do with as I will.
- Practice makes perfect.
- In 10 years', time, this will not matter.
- I deserve respect.

Cognitive Behavioral Therapy

- My thoughts do not define my reality.

- The worst-case scenario practically never occurs.

- My best will be good enough for most of the time.

- Being anxious will not prevent me from tackling this situation head on.

- I have time for me.

- I deserve a break.

- Practice, practice, practice.

- I can face the fear.

- I can choose to think different thoughts.

- I am in control of my mind.

- I deserve to feel happy.

- This is not that big of a deal; I will not let it get to me.

- Breathe deeply.

- I am in the right place, at the right time, exactly where I need to be.

- The future is not set in stone.

Rewrite Your Story

Each person is the sum of their experiences regardless if those experiences are negative or positive, or even if they are wholly unremarkable. These experiences have the power to not only shape you in the moment, but also shape every experience that comes after them based on the way they may have altered your perception of reality.

It is important to understand that everyone has their own story which means that yours is a unique sum of all the chapter your life has included to get to where you are now. While it may seem lopsided at the moment, it is also important to keep in mind that every story is bound to contain equal parts sad moments and happy ones, just as there are bound to be times that are traumatic and those that are transformational. Your story forms the core of who you are as a person which ultimately goes on to affect how you present yourself to the greater world.

Creating stories: Each day as you go about your daily activities all your experiences are filtered through your senses which then cause them to generate either a negative or positive feeling. With this done, the feeling then triggers a thought which, in turn, generates an emotion. This chain of events is then often enough to provide your mind the data it needs to broadly label the experience as something that is either positive or negative and then drilling down into any relevant specifics from there. In this sense, the emotions you have are essentially thoughts that are associated with specific physical sensations or feelings.

As these sorts of things begin to accumulate, your mind is then able to take them as a whole and assign a more generalized meaning in a broader context. As an example, if a person is put up for adoption as a baby and then experiences regular hardship as a youth as a result, they could very well end up creating a story that says their parents willing gave them up for adoption because they could tell that there was something wrong with the baby right from the start.

The specific meanings that you find in your personal experience can be thought of as threads that came together to create the tapestry that represents your entire story. As such, if you interpret your story with only negative filters, you will generate limiting beliefs that are almost certainly going to hold you back in the future. These limiting beliefs are known to manifest in a wide variety of ways, often starting with thoughts like those outlined here:

- I am not one of the specials few that deserve to be happy

- The things I can do aren't enough for me to succeed

- I'm incapable of bettering myself

- I can't do anything right

- I will never be enough

If you fill your mind with these types of limiting beliefs, negative aspects of your life such as those that are filled with fear, pain, and suffering are far more likely to reach the forefront of your mind and stay there, making it all but impossible for any positive emotions to slip through. If left untreated, this will likely leave you actively avoiding all the people and things that could potentially cause those old emotions to rise to the surface, preventing any type of real healing from taking place in the process.

The negative loop: Take a moment to consider the last time you let a negative mindset filled with self-doubt and fear stop you from taking a positive step towards a major goal. Now think about the last time you found yourself in a serious downward spiral where you had a hard time finding anything that could adequately explain what had happened. These types of behaviors are common signs of self-sabotage and are often an attempt by the subconscious to prevent you from having to deal with anything that could potentially reinforce any negative aspect of your story.

These types of subconscious motivations are referred to as unconscious drivers which are caused by unresolved emotions of varying types. While the specifics around bound to vary by person, they will revolve around certain emotions that were likely repressed at a previous point and time and thus created mental barriers that limit the types of decision your brain even remotely considers when faced with new experiences. If you feel as though you have been stuck in a rut for years, this could very well be the reason why.

Consider potential changes: While some people can think back on the bad times in their lives with ease, for others unpacking such memories is a traumatic experience all on its own. Even if they have locked their issues away, this doesn't mean they aren't there, it just means it is more difficult to determine what might uncover them. If you feel as though you are having a difficult time choosing which negative stories to change, the first thing you will need to do is take some time and reflect.

Stephen Patterson

There are three primary types of negative stories that tend to hold most people back including personal stories, stories of those close to you and stories of the world at large. As you reflect on your personal stories you will want to consider stories from each sphere and think about all the CBT progress you have made up to this point. Looking back on the biggest hurdles you had to face will often give you a clue as to where your negative stories begin.

Rewrite your story: Luckily, once you have found your negative stories you are already well on your way to changing them for the better. Understanding that you can change the narrative and changing it successfully are two very different things, however, especially as finding the best place to start can be tricky until you have had some practice. However, the best place to start is going to be by thinking about all the various ways you could potentially interpret the major events in your life.

As a rule, there are two potential types of interpretation, those that lead to a feeling of empowerment and those that lead to a sense of helplessness. As an example, imagine a pair of sisters who spent their childhoods being physically abused by their mother. Of the two, own sister seeks escape in hard drugs, fails to graduate from high school and spends her life being abused in every relationship she is ever in. The other sister, however, refused to let those negative experiences define her, excelled in college, started a career and had a loving family. Despite their identical upbringing and obviously different choices, if asked both sisters would almost certainly say that there is no way their lives could have turned out any differently.

The goal of this example is to illustrate the simple fact that everyone always has a choice when it comes to how they interpret their own story and the events, both negative and positive that have happened to you over the years. With that said, you can either choose to focus on the many negatives, which then brings to the surface things like pain and suffering; or, you have the opportunity to focus on the positive of your experience and see the opportunities that following the path you have chosen has brought you.

In order to rewrite your own story, you will first need to take a look at the many previous chapters of your life and look to the points where you feel as though an external force conspired against you to leave you worse off than you may have theoretically otherwise been. If you are still mad at your boss for skipping you over for a promotion last year, closed off to others from a bad relationship that ended years ago, or are still mad about the curveballs life has thrown you over the years then it is time to understand that the end result with such resentment is always the same and it is never productive.

While looking at your story, if you find that you are holding on to these types of old resentments then it is time to reconsider whatever it is that you are doing and thinking about what it might ultimately cost you in the long-run. If you ever want to successfully start to change your story, when looking back on these moments you will want to consider what you have learned from these experiences or how they have ultimately caused you to change and improve as a result. From there you can then think about all the other opportunities that have presented themselves to you that you would not have had if everything up to that point hadn't played out in one specific way. If given enough time you will find that by thinking about the situation in this way you are well on your way to seeing them as a positive, as opposed to a negative, event.

As you take the time to move through a greater number of your prior experiences you should find that it becomes easier and easier to find the opportunity that each new challenge really represents. Slowly but surely, you should find that you are able to look back at your life as a whole and see it all in a new light. Never forget,

Cognitive Behavioral Therapy

hardship is a part of every story, the only things that make your story unique is the way you define it.

Stephen Patterson

Chapter 5:
Techniques for Dealing with Anxiety

If it is your insecurities that are causing issues, you may need to work on whatever is causing that in your life. Just because someone says something or constructively critiques you at work doesn't mean that you can just lose yourself to anxiety. Learning how to deal with these insecurities, or even what is causing those insecurities, can make a big difference in how you will react to others.

Socratic questioning. In order to get started you are going to want to practice what is known as Socratic questioning. Based on the teachings of the Greek philosopher Socrates, the goal of this exercise is to use questions to explore complicated ideas in order to uncover the inherent assumptions they are based upon. Using his method will allow you to determine if you are looking at something through a cognitive bias filter using several questions such as:

- Is my reaction in this situation based on the specifics of what is going on around me or is it just an automatic reaction?

- Am I looking at this situation as black and white when it is really some shade of gray?

- Is the thought I'm considering based on any hard evidence?

- Is this thought coming from a place of facts or feelings?

- Is the thought I'm having realistic?

While you may be tempted to rush through the questions, especially early on, it is important to remember that they are here for you to use as they can help you, they are not some meaningless ritual you blow through as quickly as possible just to say you've done it. Rather you are going to want to spend a few minutes really thinking through each question in order to be sure you can come up with the best answer possible. With practice, you will find that you are able to move through the questions more easily and that the time you do take to consider them will give you the time you need to think before you react to a negative scenario, decreasing the likelihood that you will take actions that will lead to negative feelings later on.

Decatastrophizing: After your Socratic questioning leads you to at least one relevant cognitive distortion you will then need to practice a process called *decatastrophizing* to make sure that you can deal with them and leave them properly stored. As they become easier to spot, you will often find that your cognitive distortions reflect reality accurately, expect that one aspect is often extremely skewed.

For example, if you are someone who frequently has anxiety attacks, then prior to going on a date with someone new you may be stuck with crippling anxiety thinking about how the other person might not like you, how you will likely have nothing to talk about and all the ways you may potentially embarrass yourself. When scenarios like these are running through your head you will find that if you take the time to really think the situation through you will generally find that the potential consequences aren't nearly as dire as you may have thought from the start.

As such, if you find yourself in a situation where you feel yourself spiraling out of control then all you really need to do is to stop and take some time to mull over the absolute worse-case scenario that could occur if everything suddenly went wrong at once. As this will rarely end with you losing life or limb, taking the time to practice this exercise is often enough time to allow you to realize that you were overreacting.

Returning to the dating scenario, if you are nervous about how poorly you are now sure the date is going to go, if you take the time to think things through to the end then you will see that you don't have much to worry about. After all, it is impossible to die from embarrassment which means the worst thing that can happen is the date ends early and you never see the other person again, which isn't so bad in the grand scheme of things.

If you make a habit of using this technique you are bound to find that a vast majority of the things that you used to spend so much time obsessing over aren't all that serious. This should naturally give you a push to start taking an even closer look at your cognitive distortions which is the first step to one day breaking through them. At the very least it should be enough to snap you out of it in the moment while also making it more likely you can avoid these issues in the future.

Hold a trial for your negative thoughts: Another useful exercise when it comes to confronting your cognitive distortions head on is putting them on trial. With this exercise you literally act as dense, prosecutor and jury for each cognitive distortion you come across in order to determine if it holds water. To begin, you will want to take the side of the defense and hold up any positive aspects of the cognitive distortion you are taking a closer look at. To do so you will need to think of any arguments as to why the thought is true and anything that points to it being the right response to have in certain situations. While acting as the defense it is important to only look at the facts and nothing but the facts as letting any type of conjecture into the proceedings will only end up mucking up the results.

Once you rest as the defense, the next thing you will want to do is to act as the prosecution and come up with every single reason you can think of as to why the cognitive distortion is not only false but harmful to your everyday state of mind. You will need to present an airtight case if you hope to push past the cognitive distortion for good, however, as any guesswork or opinion at this point in the process will only give your mind reasons to cling to the distortion in the future.

After you have presented all the facts on both sides, it is important to then act as the jury to see which arguments are the most valid. If the defense comes out on top, then you may not actually be looking at a cognitive distortion at all and you can move forward as such. Assuming the prosecution comes out ahead, which is what is bound to happen most of the time, then you can start down the road to clearing up the distortion once and for all.

Consider the accuracy of your thoughts: After you have come up with a list of the cognitive distortions that are causing you the most grief, the next thing you will need to do is test each of the distortions to ensure they are actually not reflecting reality in any meaningful way. As an example, if you find that you spend far too much time worrying about problems that may not even come to pass as a way of ensuring you will always have a solution ready, then you will want to put this theory to the test.

To do so you may then spend a week or two tracking the amount of time you spend trying to deal with problems that ultimately don't materialize so you can decide if there is a better way to spend that time with a much specific detail in front of you as possible. If it turns out there is nothing more you can do then great, now you know you are on the right track; if that is not the case, however, then you can quickly take more steps to correct it.

Behaviorally testing your thought: Depending on the cognitive distortion you are dealing with you might possible be able to disprove it by taking matters more directly into your own hands. As an example, if you feel as though you are more productive throughout the day if you don't take any breaks, you could spend a week working as you see fit and then rating your productivity at the end of each day. You could then take a second week and take more breaks, before then rating yourself at the end of each day as well. Assuming your cognitive distortion isn't so extreme that it has moved on into full delusion territory then if you are directly faced with the inaccuracy of a thought it will be moved towards positive change.

Self-Hypnosis

Subjecting yourself to hypnosis will allow you to enter an enhanced state of extreme focus whereby you will be able to quiet your stream of consciousness and focus all your attention on a single thought. Achieving this state is easier as children but becomes difficult as we age because the mind slowly fills with deep rooted thoughts and beliefs which are more difficult to pierce using hypnosis.

This process is effective because thoughts that are introduced into the subconscious make their way to the conscious part of the mind and manifest themselves as the desire to act on a specific topic. Consider it this way, the subconscious provides the impetus towards action, the conscious mind provides the will to see it through. Without this motivation, positive thoughts remain only that which is why self-hypnosis can be so beneficial when it comes to creating new habits.

Now that you have a basic understanding of how self-hypnosis works and why it is time to learn how to create appropriate hypnotic suggestions for yourself to insert into the scripts in the later chapters for when you record your own hypnotic suggestion audio files. Remember, hypnotic suggestions can fundamentally alter the way you think, use them with caution.

it is important to formulate your autosuggestions properly to ensure that they make it to your subconscious. The two primary traits of a good autosuggestion are that it is positive and that it is focused on a specific goal. Besides these main goals, what follows are a few extra ways of improving your autosuggestions' effectiveness.

Make each autosuggestion a certainty. Formulate your thoughts using full sentences that indicate the change you are hoping for has already occurred. Remember, the subconscious has trouble distinguishing between imagination and reality, use this to your advantage.

Ensure your autosuggestions contain clear goals. Your subconscious won't know what to plan on doing if you don't give it the firm

Cognitive Behavioral Therapy

direction it needs. A good autosuggestion takes a held belief and matches with a positive goal to ensure the best success.

Use the present tense: When formulating your goals always write in the present and refer to goals as close at hand. The hypnotic suggestion will give you the conviction you need to reach difficult goals.

If you suffer from chronic nervousness or anxiety attacks this script will help you rewire the way your brain thinks while also implanting a coping device to use in the moment when life begins to overwhelm you.

Begin

At the sound of my voice, you will find your body becoming extremely relaxed.

<Pause>

Your heart is slowing down; your palms will soon stop sweating.

<Pause>

From now on you will naturally be calmer and less anxious because you know there is nothing to be anxious about and that your life will always work out for the best.

\<Pause\>
You know this is the case because you are a winner and a winning mindset is strong enough to hold back any negative emotion. You oversee how you feel, and nothing can change that.

\<Pause\>
Using just the power of your mind you can accomplish all your goals and ensure that all your dreams come true.

\<Pause\>
Everything is right in the world and life is proceeding as it should.

\<Pause\>
You are a winner and that means you should not bother being afraid, anxious or worried, winners always win so there is nothing worth bothering yourself about.

\<Pause\>
Visualize your anxiety as a physical cloth that is covering your head and making it difficult for you to see. Picture yourself pulling the cloth off your body and stuffing into a chest before locking it up tight.

Cognitive Behavioral Therapy

<Pause>

With you face clear you will now be able to see your problems as they approach and face them with confidence and the freedom to make the best choices based on the situation.

<Pause>

Visualize the chest locking with the words Relaxation and Peace inscribed on the lock. These two words will now be enough to trigger a physical response in your body. Seeing these two words emblazoned across your mental landscape will now be enough to stop your body from being anxious and clear your mind of stress and down.

<Pause>

Relaxation and Peace will now send you into a state of complete relaxation that not even the strongest anxiety attack can overcome.

<Pause>

Relaxation and Peace are now all you need to overcome all mental obstacles that you will ever encounter.

<Pause>
Relaxation and Peace will now be the trigger that helps your mind close its doors on any negative thoughts or emotions.

<Pause>
Keep Relaxation and Peace at the forefront of your mind and everything else will be perpetually in your grasp.

<Pause>
Now take three long, deep breaths and feel your fears and stress melting away. 1...2...3...

<Pause>
Breathe in.... breathe out and as you do so feel any remaining tension leaving your body.

<Pause>
Breathe in and hold your breath before mindfully exhaling.

<Pause>
Feel additional layers of relaxation drift over you as you breathe in and out.

Cognitive Behavioral Therapy

<Pause>

Visualize yourself outside under a beautiful night sky.

<Pause>

Picture a brilliant star hanging above you in the heavens spinning and spinning and spinning.

<Pause>

You have complete control over the star, spin it in any direction that you wish.

<Pause>

As the start spins, feel yourself becoming still more relaxed, more relaxed than you even knew was possible.

<Pause>

You can feel no anxiety, worry or fear while operating the star, only peace, and happiness.

<Pause>

You are in complete control of your universe; your mind feels focused and fit.

Stephen Patterson

\<Pause\>

Let the star go and instead picture yourself in a place that you feel extremely safe and comfortable. The safest, most secure place you can possibly imagine.

\<Pause\>

Picture this place in detail, imagine how it looks, feels, smells, even how the air tastes when you are there. Now picture the words Relaxation and Peace writ large upon this safe space.

\<Pause\>

Imagine how safe you are in this moment in your most secure spot and then know that this level of security will follow you back to the real world.

\<Pause\>

Internalize that feeling as completely as possible, hold onto it and never let it go.

\<Pause\>

There are no fears, no worries, nothing to get anxious about at all. There is only the feeling you have in your safe place.

Cognitive Behavioral Therapy

<Pause>
Insert 3 minutes of calming music

<Pause>
Remember Relaxation and Peace are linked to your safe space, moving forward thinking about them will let you access your feeling of complete security which will overwrite any negative feelings you might have.

<Pause>
You are completely relaxed from your toes to your nose.

<Pause>
Your eyes are growing tired even as your mind is waking up.

<Pause>
Take a series of three deep breaths and with each, you will find that you feel fuller of energy and more ready to face the tasks ahead whatever they may be.

<Pause>

Stephen Patterson

I will now count backward from three and when I do you will awaken completely rejuvenated and no longer the least bit anxious or afraid.

<Pause>

3...2...1...

End

Once you have recorded your audio autosuggestions and are prepared to start a session of self-hypnosis the next step is to prepare your body to enter a trance-like state. This state will allow you to focus all your concentration on the autosuggestions you have chosen and is most commonly associated with hypnotic practices.

Much like hypnosis itself, the word trance can have negative connotations that ignore the fact that free will is never taken out of the equation. A trance only increases focus, what you do with that focus is up to you. Likewise, the ability to control which suggestions you listen to is a skill in and of itself which means you will become more proficient at it in time. This means you will be able to more easily accept new autosuggestions you like while easily fighting off those you do not.

In order to ensure that self-hypnosis it is effective, it is important that you take the time before you start to have a conversation with yourself about the reasons behind the habit or life choice you are trying to change. Another issue that can create resistance is that those who try self-hypnosis have built up unrealistic expectations as to what it entails. Put aside all your expectations as to what a hypnotic trance may involve, and you will find it much easier to achieve the desired results.

There won't be any half-conscious episodes or feelings of lightness or floating. Hopefully, you will feel a little more aware of your surroundings and find it easier to focus on the sound of your own voice but otherwise, that's it. While it may not feel like much, your senses and your mind will be heightened during this time and primed for suggestion.

When you first begin using hypnotherapy it is important to conduct sessions for at least 20 minutes at a time. Ideally, 2 sessions per day should be the goal as the extra repetition will help the autosuggestions enter your subconscious more efficiently. After you have been using self-hypnosis for long enough that your subconscious has become accustomed to accepting autosuggestions you can generally reduce your sessions without losing efficacy.

Chapter 6:
Techniques for Dealing with Fear

Exposure Therapy

Exposure therapy is a type of CBT that is often used to deal with issues relating to the responses generated by either fear or anxiety-inducing incidents. While in guided therapy you will likely be exposed to a variation of whatever it is that makes you afraid or anxious until the negative response has been lessened to the point it no longer presents a problem. There are also several types of exercises you can work through on your own.

Interoceptive exposure: This type of exposure therapy is particularly effective for those who are dealing with fear or anxiety related to feeling specific bodily sensations. Avoiding these sensations then leads to biased behaviors based on biased beliefs which then lead to avoidance behaviors. As such, exposure to these types of bodily sensations, known as interoceptive exposure can be an important part of treatment, especially when it comes to panic disorders.

To practice dealing with the issues that sensations call forth, practice the following.

Breathing
- Rapidly breathe in and out, taking full breathes each time (1 minute)

- Hold your nose and breathe through a straw (2 minutes)

- Hold your breath (30 seconds)

Physical Exercise
- Run in place (2 minutes)

- Walk up and down the stairs (2 minutes)

- Tense all the muscles in your body (1 minute)

Spinning or Shaking
- Spin as fast as you can while sitting in an office chair (1 minute)

- Spin while standing as fast as you can (1 minute)

- Shake your head back and forth before looking straight ahead (30 seconds)

- Put your head between your legs and then stand up quickly (1 minute)

- Lie down for a minute and then stand up quickly (1 minute)

Unreality
- Stare at yourself in a mirror (2 minutes)

- Stare at a blank wall (2 minutes)

- Stare at a florescent light and then read something (1 minute)

Imagery based exposure: The goal with imagery-based exposure therapy is for you to react to scenes that are presented to you in such a way that you feel as though they are occurring. While you might be surprised to find that a picture can have such a severe effect on your behavior, with the right preparation you will be surprised at how easily they can induce anxiety. This type of exposure therapy has proven to be extremely effective in helping those who deal with generalized anxiety disorder.

Imagery based exposure is particularly effective for those who find themselves ruminating on events in the past and building up their overall level of anxiety in the process. As a result, it can be especially effective when it comes to reducing the need to avoid high anxiety situations thanks to a lack of any other useful coping mechanisms.

One version of this exercise is done by simply thinking of a recent experience that you have had that caused extremely strong feelings of anxiety to materialize. As an example, if you recently gave a presentation at work that led to serious issues on your part, you could then recall that situation later in your mind to turn the traumatic event into a positive. Luckily, it is most likely that you can remember the least positive experiences you have so putting yourself right back in the moment should only be the work of a few minutes.

As an example, you would want to start by remembering how the room looked, what your supervisor was wearing and where all your coworkers were sitting. You will then want to consider the way it felt when you were in the room, the sounds you heard during the presentation, anything specific that you can possibly remember in order to return yourself as completely to the moment as possible.

Nightmare re-scripting: This type of expose therapy is useful for those who have specific intense fears by allowing them to be faced head on, thus removing any power they hold over you. Nightmare exposure typically goes hand in hand with a technique known as re-scripting which is often used as a way of helping those who are suffering from severely stressful memories by changing the way they are perceived. It can be effective regardless if the memory that is being re-scripted is something that happened in real life as opposed to something that only occurs in the nebulous realm of dreams.

Re-scripting is also beneficial when it comes to attempting to deal with the types of everyday negative experiences that regularly lead to frustration and sadness. Studies even show that this technique can be employed to significantly reduce the frequency of any related nightmares assuming it is used properly and on a strict schedule until results are achieved.

To begin making use of this technique, the next time you have a nightmare related to your issues, don't simply brush it under the rug the next morning. Instead, you will want to challenge it and confront what it might mean by considering various aspects of your dream.

For starters, you will want to focus on the worst part of the dream, the part that you would naturally shy away from the most. While this will likely be a difficult thing to face head on, the only way you can ever expect to really change your dreams is if they are more fully understood. Even if you have been having the same dream for years, you will want to start by writing it all down as it will help you to put a logic to it that is often difficult to parse while you are experiencing it firsthand. You will also want to apply the same cadre of descriptive methods to it that you would to any real-life experiences that might be causing it.

Fake It

Specifically, you may find that faking a degree of confidence that you don't yet feel can be an extremely effective way to improve social interactions of all types, without having to have fully deal with the issues that may be at the root of your lack of confidence. While this might sound ridiculous, take a moment and consider a scenario where you were interacting with a person who you identify as being supremely confident. Now consider all the things about this person that made you believe they were confident and ask yourself how would you have known if they were faking it?

Cognitive Behavioral Therapy

The truth of the matter is that if you act confidently in each situation then those around you will have no reason to assume you feel otherwise. As such, pretending to have confidence and being confident are two sides of the same coin. What's more, having success when pretending to have confidence once, will make it much easier to do a second time, and what's more, each additional time you pretend to have confidence you will have to pretend less and less until you won't be pretending at all.

Acting confident: In order to act the way a confident person would act in a given situation, all you need to do is to visualize someone you know who is confident and then ask yourself what they would do if they were in your position. From there, it is just a matter of following their lead. Think about the way they would present themselves, what type of gestures they would use, what type of body language they would utilize and how they would speak. With a good role model to follow you will be surprised at how easy playing pretend can be.

Be aware of your image: Confident people are naturally more outgoing, happier and friendlier to those they meet. It is then easier to project an aura of confidence by simply acting friendly to those you meet, smiling regularly and taking the initiative in conversations.

Find a confidence role model: When it comes to acting like you are confident, it is as easy as taking the time to consider the person who you consider to be more self-confident than anyone else you know. With a clear image in your mind, you are going to want to then ask yourself how the person in question would approach the conversation you are about to have. The more specific you can be when it comes to actions and mannerisms the better; this means things like body language, patterns of speech and conversational habits. Put yourself into your role model's headspace as completely as possible and then do what they would do.

Approach with a purpose: Those with an appropriate level of self-confidence tend to walk everywhere they go with a purpose. When you approach someone new, this means you are going to want to do so with your head held back and your shoulders squared. If you present, yourself while slumped over and slouching you are telling the other person that you do not have confidence in yourself and that they should not either. You will also want to walk a little more quickly than normal to indicate that you are someone who knows where they need to be.

Be complementary: Self-confident individuals can more easily see the good in those around them because they are familiar with what's great about themselves as well. This means that approaching confidently and then following that up by starting a conversation with a complement and a follow up question is a one-two punch that virtually guarantees the other person will remember you as someone who is confident in themselves and their abilities.

Consider how starting a conversation makes you seem: Self-confident individuals are typically considered friendlier and more outgoing than their peers. As such, simply by being the one to make the first contact with a stranger, automatically makes them perceive you as being more confident than they are. This knowledge should then make it even easier for you to act self-confident as you are acting to an audience that has already been convinced. Taking the time to always introduce yourself to people you haven't met before, even if you don't then initiate conversation will let them know that you know you are a person with value who deserves respect.

Behavioral activation: If rather than experiencing a specific type of fear, you instead feel a more generalized version that is always present, then behavioral activation may be the right choice. The idea behind this exercise is that if you experience enough negative events during childhood then you may have missed out on the positive reinforcement that allows you to act appropriately in many different situations. If left untreated, this has the potential to lead to feelings of fear that are completely off base, a general desire to withdraw from the world and a host of other erratic behaviors.

If any of this sounds familiar than the best way to deal with this specific type of issue is to attempt to counteract the negative buildup and an easy way to do that is to find a hobby that you are good at and then find a venue to show it off to a group. While this might be enough to cause some people to feel terrified, you can counteract this potential by choosing something that you are sure you won't be able to screw up. Once you go through with your plan you will be well on your way to generating the type of positive reinforcement you have likely been looking for most of your life. While not everyone is going to have a skill or hobby that is suited to this type of performance right off the bat, this exercise isn't limited to traditional types of performances, any type of demonstration of your skills should be seriously considered.

If you still feel as though you have no worthwhile skills, take your time and don't sell yourself short. Keep in mind that everyone has some skills that set them apart and just because yours aren't flashy doesn't mean there isn't a perfectly acceptable way out there to show off what you do to those who really appreciate it. Take some time and seek out forums related to your chosen niche online and you will often find an easy way to display your talent to those who are sure to appreciate it.

This doesn't have to be something serious like jumping up on stage and starting a band, there is any number of ways you can count on your skills being appreciated. As an example, if you are good at planning events then you could volunteer to help a local charity plan a fundraiser. This way you not only help to ensure that the event is a success, you get to show off your skills in the process. Similarly, if you are an excellent cook but live alone, invite your friends over for dinner once a week, they are sure to take you up on the offer.

Finally, once you find an activity that serves to really boost your personal confidence level, the last step is going to be keeping it up regularly to help your mind learn to expect the positives instead of the negatives. While being given praise will likely do little to decrease your fear at first, you will be surprised how effective having confidence in just one section of your life can spread to the others. Once you find a reliable positive outlet for your skill you should find that utilizing positive reinforcement on a regular basis can make you forget all about your fear.

Stephen Patterson

Chapter 7:
Techniques for Dealing with Depression

Developing an attitude of optimism is great for your mind, body, and spirit. However, it isn't easy to be all positive and upbeat in all circumstances, especially if you've been through a series of tough situations. It can be challenging to keep upkeep a positive attitude all the time. Here are some of the most powerful and effective tips to make positive thinking your second nature.

Be aware of negative self-talk: While most people probably won't admit it, everyone talks to themselves in one way or another. Even if it is just an inner monologue and less of a conversation, this inner voice is always with you which means it is important to ensure it is saying the right things. If this voice says negative things it can easily affect your self-confidence in a serious way which is why the first thing you want to do is to keep an eye out for when it is saying negative things.

The first step towards fixing the problem is being aware of it, if you have already practiced meditation than the concept of seeing thoughts without interacting with them will already be familiar to you. Basically, what you want to do is take the time to become fully aware of every thought that passes through your mind. Common forms of negative self-talk involve the phrases "I can't" or "I have never been able to", these are common answers to fixed mindset patterns and should be avoided at all costs. If you find you mind being full of these sorts of statements respond to them by asking "why can't I" and see where this train of thought leads you.

It can be easy to let thoughts exist in the background while another task is front and center but for this exercise, it is important to focus on those other thoughts for long enough to ensure that they aren't harboring thoughts which might promote a fixed mindset. The trick is hearing these thoughts without interacting with them, the goal is to find them and let them go without giving them any extra mental real estate. While you are working on not interacting with these disruptive thoughts it can be helpful to instead think "Abort, abort" after any negative self-talk has been perceived. This command will break up whatever thought process you were currently working through and allow you to eject the negative thought more easily.

Cognitive Behavioral Therapy

Stop playing the victim: It is easy to play victim and blame circumstances when you encounter challenges in life. However, when you learn to accept reasonability for your behavior, you learn from your mistakes and display greater control over future circumstances. Avoid blaming other people unfairly. Admit your mistake and move on. Some things cannot be changed, which means we simply accept them and move on.

Though we cannot control each situation befalling us, we can control our reaction to the situation. Rather than playing the victim, simply acknowledge the circumstances and realize that you are in control of your reaction. Control the things you can and learn to let go of what you can't. Playing victim makes you feel more helpless and less in control. Break the shackles of helplessness to take greater control of your life, which ultimately leads to increased positivity and happiness. Be the ultimate "possibilitarian" you can.

Do not wait for situations to change. Act as they have already changed even when you feel victimized by circumstances. Believe that the power to shift your circumstances doesn't lie externally but is held within you. If you are looking for love, begin loving yourself unconditionally first. If you are looking for a new job, make the most of the one you are currently working in. Understand that the process of change begins with your intention to change the circumstances surrounding you.

Stop making excuses: You either have a dream or an excuse. They can't co-exist. There can be a zillion excuses for not achieving something or not doing things that make you happy. What is stopping you? Quit giving excuses. Sign up for those dance lessons today.

Start saving to travel the world. Go out there and make friends if your previous relationship ended on a disastrous note. Life is about living, not coming up with a bunch of excuses for simply existing. Are you truly living or merely existing? Don't create obstacles in your path to happiness. Ditch them and go out there to live a life you've always dreamt of.

Spend time with positive folks: Did you know that your attitude and personality reflect the 5 people you spend maximum time with? Research has proven that the attitude, beliefs, thoughts, and outlook of the people we spend most of our waking hours with has a huge impact on us. When you are surrounded by habitual complainers and whiners, you won't be able to escape their negativity.

Cognitive Behavioral Therapy

Choose the people in your immediate circle carefully. Spend time with positive and inspiring folks, who show an attitude of gratitude. Their habits and thinking will become your thoughts and behavior. It is virtually impossible to be negative when it's all rainbow and sunshine around you.

When you fill your life with positive folks, you'll keep hearing positive stories, affirmations, and thoughts. These words and feelings will sink into your psyche to influence your own thoughts, which eventually affect your words and actions. Eliminate negativity from your spirit before it completely takes over.

Accept responsibility for your actions: Avoid blaming others or circumstances for the problems you encounter. Successful people rarely play victims of circumstances. Accept complete responsibility for your behavior. Admit you made a mistake rather than making someone else the scapegoat for your actions. When you accept responsibility for your actions, you take a brave step towards learning from your mistakes. Give credit to others wherever due. Do no blame them unfairly.

Practice high self-care standards: Take good care of yourself if you want to think and feel more positive. It is hard to be negative from within when you are healthy and glowing from the outside. Pursue an enjoyable and fulfilling physical activity to stay fit. Eat a balanced and healthy diet. Maintain superior hygiene standards. Wear clean clothes. Keep up a well-groomed appearance. When you look and feel confident, there is a greater tendency to approach everything with positivity.

Appreciate moments when everything goes right: Another good way to ensure that your self-talk remains positive is to take time to stop and smell the roses. While this may sound trite, taking the time to appreciate these moments and really experience them will all your senses. Then, the next time you find yourself beset by negative self-talk simply counter it with the belief that things will get better and then use one of your stored memories as proof. What's more, making the conscious effort to fill your head with happy positive thoughts will eventually make it less likely that negative self-talk will occur as your neural pathways shift into a growth mindset.

Remember, like the other mental reprograming tricks discussed in previous chapters, changing the tone of your self-talk won't happen overnight. Keep out it however as the results will surprise you. As your self-talk turns from critic to cheerleader you will find that you feel a greater sense of personal fulfilment, peace, and happiness while at the same time feeling more empowered to reach your goals.

Anchoring: Anchoring is going to assist in forcing the user to fall into an emotion that is not negative or into a frame of mind that is positive. Anchoring is usually associated with gestures, words, or even touching an object so that the user can anchor themselves to that emotion and recall it later.

When using this technique, one way that it can be used is to recall a memory that made you very happy. This time can be something simple such as winning a sports game, or it can be something big like getting married or when your child/children were born.

As you remember the moments that lead up to this happy moment, recall every detail that you can so that you can relive the story and bring that feeling forward as vividly as possibly.

While recalling the memory, you should take your right hand and squeeze your index and middle fingers together quickly two times in a row. During that second squeeze, the image that you have drawn forth needs to overtake your mental image so that you can cause the feeling that you are having to intensify.

Whenever you recall that memory, either to yourself or to someone else, each time that you squeeze those fingers together now, the feeling is going to keep growing. However, you are going to have to repeat this process several times so that you can get your body to realize what you are training it to do.

But this is not the only way that you are going to create an anchor to a happy feeling that you can call upon when things get tough. As you progress through using this technique, you are going to use this same method so that you can recall this feeling and not have to worry about it not working.

The anchoring method will aid you in associating the two squeezes of your fingers with the feeling of being happy. Being that the more you practice, the easier things get, the same is true with this strategy.

Pattern interruption: While using the pattern interruption technique, key words are going to be placed into someone's mind on an unconscious level. This is a good technique that can be used with anchoring. Using pattern interruption, someone is going to be drawn in by an inner monologue or their train of thought that happens to follow a pattern that they may not realize is going on. Your unconsciousness is going to anxiously anticipate the next part of the pattern even if the part of the mind that you can control is preoccupied with something else.

The purpose behind pattern technique is to get someone to forget about what they were doing in the first place and get them to do something different. The subconscious part of the mind is going to know that other tasks have not been completed, but it is not going to be able to do the tasks that need to be done because it has no control over what the body does.

Affirmations and mantras: Depression is often triggered by the way you perceive that specific events have taken place in the past as well as what you feel as though the future will most certainly bring. These perceptions can, in turn, be influenced by the filters that your mind has built up as a means of organizing the world around it. Unfortunately, all the data your mind must go in is based on your previous experiences which means it is quite easy for it to be biased in one way or another. Thus, if you experience enough negativity up front, it makes it difficult to ever remove that filter and you will have a hard time seeing any type of positivity anywhere.

As a matter of fact, if your depression gets bad enough your filters could even go so far as to remove any positive benefits that you might get from positive activities or other exercises you may try or otherwise experience throughout the day. This then serves to compound the problem even more and can cause you to feel as though you have no real way to move forward in a productive fashion, regardless of what the case might be.

Therefore, affirmations and mantras can be so effective as the repetition that they both uses is an excellent way to sneak positive thoughts past your negative filters, allowing your mind to get in touch with new insight that it might otherwise never experience. An affirmation is any positive thought that is written down throughout the day. A mantra works in much the same way expect that you simply think the positive sentence as opposed to writing it down. With enough practice, you will find that both activities are a great way to get your brain primed for forming new neural pathways that will help to bypass these filters entirely.

- Useful affirmations or mantras to try to include:

- *Today, you are perfect*

- *Forward progress! Just keep moving!*

Cognitive Behavioral Therapy

- *You are the sky*

- *I am attracting all the love I dream of and deserve*

- *Follow my path to happiness*

- *I am strong. I am beautiful. I am enough*

- *I am grateful for my life so far and for what is to come*

- *I am fulfilled*

- *You were born with potential, you were born with goodness and trust, you were born with ideals and dreams, you were born with greatness, you were born with wings, you were not meant for crawling so don't, you have wings, learn to use them and fly.*

- *I am righteous and truthful to myself and others and about myself and others, my soul is whole, my family, community, and environment are order and are stable, and I am in balance with the natural world.*

- *When things don't go your way, when things go "wrong", and especially if you do not seem to currently have enough money, do not attach a story or sense of self-worth to your circumstances.*

- *Changing your life is hard. Changing your perception in which you see your world is easy. What are you waiting for? Get started!*

When you first get started, it will be perfectly natural for your mind to fight back against these unfamiliar thoughts, simply because they are so much different than the way it typically experiences the world. This is a perfectly natural part of the process, however, as you are working hard to actively change the way your primary mental filters have worked for years so it is only natural there is some pushback. If you keep at it and continue moving in the right direction you will eventually get where you need to be.

You will know if you are on the right track if you can hear your mantra running continuously in the back of your head, even when you are not actively thinking about it. When writing your affirmations down, trying and write them at least three times per day in sets of five.

Think about your core beliefs: If you have been dealing with depression for many years then it is entirely possible that some facet of your core belief system may be fundamentally incongruous with the way the world works. The first step in ensuring that this is no longer the case, while also decreasing your overall emotional state in the process, is to determine what mental agreements are coming into play. These mental agreements typically come in bundles which means that if you take the time to identify the package of beliefs that you are interacting with, you will be well on your way to changing them which will be covered in tomorrow's exercise.

As with many of the exercises discussed in these pages, it may be difficult to pull off correctly at first but will get easier with practice. In order to get started effectively, you may find it useful to think of uncovering a core belief as akin to solving a mystery which means you need to get to look at the clues that are left in place by your subconscious.

It is important to learn to distinguish these types of thoughts from core beliefs as your thoughts are not to be trusted if you are dealing with an extreme level of depression. When it comes to tracking down the core belief that is causing you distress now, the best way to continue digging deeper is to follow the emotions that you are having in response. You will want to continue to question how your emotions are being influenced by external events to get to the core belief that is truly pulling the strings.

Once you have determined the core beliefs that are causing your issues, the next step is going to be banishing them from your thought processes once and for all. While the deeply internalized nature of the belief, can be a difficult nut to crack, you can begin softening it up by first considering the way you deal with the assumptions of others.

Most importantly, this means understanding that you cannot ever be exactly how people see you in their heads. While somewhat of a letdown, this idea should be largely mitigated by the fact that you can't ever truly know what another person is thinking so you will never know what you are up against. This is an easy truth to come to, after all, you are not a mind reader; nevertheless, it is powerful in that it puts some space to work in the set of beliefs that are tied directly to the core belief you are going to change. Becoming aware of the limits of your beliefs can make them much easier to change.

However, this is not to say that you need to change all the related agreements for a given belief all at once, and indeed that is likely asking more than the average person can deliver. Rather, you may find it helpful to think of each individual agreement as its own link in the chain of the core belief which means that the more links you weaken, the harder it will be for the chain to ultimately remain intact.

With that in mind, one of the best places to start is with the belief that just because someone else thinks something about you, that thought must be true. This is an associated link in a great many chains that many people assume to be true without a second thought, yet clearly falls apart when given any degree of true consideration. While it is true that everyone will always have opinions, a shocking number of these are uninformed or underinformed which means they are, at best, likely to be right just 50 percent of the time. When you consider the fact that everyone is also operating under their own mental filters and cognitive distortions it becomes surprising that anyone ever has a valid opinion period.

After you can make the leap and understand that there is more to you than just what other people believe, you will find that many of your beliefs that revolve around others start to fall apart as well. After all, if you are more than someone else's mental concept of you then the things that those people think become much less relevant in your daily life.

Stephen Patterson

After you reach this point you should be able to finally realize that changing a core belief is actually quite a bit easier than you originally thought, all that is required is for you to stop believing in the old version of the belief and substitute it for a new one instead. The only thing left for you to do is learn to identify them which you should find is something that gets easier each time that you manage to do so successfully. With practice you will find that you really are able to change your core beliefs for the better, transforming your point of view in the process.

Chapter 8:
Additional Steps to Take

Sleep Better

When it comes to ensuring your time spent practicing CBT is as productive as possible, one of the first things you need to do is ensure you are getting the best night's sleep possible. Unfortunately, while almost everyone is interested in getting a better night's sleep, actively taking steps to reliably do so can be surprisingly difficult. Consider the following tips and you will be getting a better night's sleep before you know it.

Unplug: While it might seem surprising, one of the easiest ways to improve both the quantity and quality of sleep that you receive is to remove all the electronics from your bedroom. This is the case for many reasons, the first of which is the fact that the blue light emitted from computers, tablets, smartphones, and televisions suppress the amount of melatonin that the body produces. Melatonin plays a large role in the regulation of circadian rhythms which make it easier to both fall asleep and stay asleep once you are. As such, removing these devices, and replacing the alarm on your phone with a good old-fashioned alarm clock is a great first step.

Exercise regularly: Studies show that exercising regularly is helpful when it comes to making your body feel ready for sleep. This doesn't need to be a full-fledged workout, something as simple as a 20-minute walk around the block can be enough to get your blood moving and improve the quality of your sleep as a result. With, it is important to finish at least 2 hours prior to hitting the hay to give your body plenty of time to wind down and prepare for sleep after the fact.

Get into a routine: Studies show that a full 75 percent of all adults don't go to bed at the same time every night. If you are looking to get a better night's sleep, then setting up a schedule and getting your body into the habit of sleeping for a set period is a great way to do so. After just two weeks of adopting a regular sleep schedule, most people not only report that it is easier for them to fall asleep, they also report sleeping better overall as well.

While the techniques discussed in this chapter don't technically fall under the umbrella of CBT, they all involve core CBT principals and will also make it easier for you to make it through your other exercises more effectively.

Improve Your Emotional Intelligence

How does emotional quotient differ from intelligence quotient? The simple answer is- they measure different forms of intelligence. Your technical acumen or technical skills is a direct result of a high intelligence quotient. You've mastered your skills well, which reflects well-developed cognitive abilities. However, is intelligent quotient enough to determine your success when it comes to dealing with people (unless you are cooped up on a remote island all yourself, you must deal with people)?

While intelligence quotient measures your technical expertise, emotional quotient evaluates your ability to manage your and other people's emotions in your work and personal life. You know where every employee stands when it comes to technical prowess, but do you really understand their thoughts, actions, and feelings to be able to better manage your and their behavior in sync with these emotions. When we gain insights into the underlying emotional patterns of people, it becomes easier to relate to them and channelize more productive behavior. This is a fundamental difference between intelligence quotient and emotional quotient.

Ever wondered why some of the cleverest people hit a blank in their professional lives and just can't seem to climb the corporate ladder, while the less knowledgeable and inexperienced folks smoothly sail their way to professional success? We all know of people who don't exactly possess the slickest technical skills yet surprisingly manage to reach top management positions. What is it that sets them apart from their more technically competent peers? Emotional intelligence is the key. It is their ability to recognize and control their and other's emotions to build more productive relationships that helps them reach their full potential.

A person's intelligence quotient demonstrates their core technical competencies, cognitive development, and unusual abilities, their emotional intelligence determines their ability to identify emotions and deal with others. Your emotional quotient determines how you will deal with stress, difficult people, bullying, high pressure work situations, conflict within the team, and differences in relationships.

There are so many theories on Emotional Intelligence, why it's important and how it can be used. However, there are a few key elements to EQ that seem to be found in every discussion. According to EQ guru Daniel Goleman, there are five key elements to EQ:

- Self-awareness

- Self-regulation

- Motivation

- Empathy

- Social skills

These buzzwords are agreed on across the board. The first, and arguably most important, element is self-awareness since without knowing and understanding yourself, your own emotions, your triggers, etc., how can you perform any self-assessment to grow or improve? Correctly identifying your own emotions is the basis for EQ.

Self-regulation comes from self-awareness. Once you are in sync with your own emotions and understand when and why you feel them, you can then regulate them. In other words, if you know that you get very angry when someone talks down to you, you can prepare yourself to preemptively disrupt your anger.

Thinking before acting is key in controlling emotions as well as withholding judgement of others. Most people tend to react in emotionally intense situations, having angry outbursts when something goes wrong or taking constructive criticism personally to the point of becoming depressed. People also tend to judge others before trying to understand why that person is saying, doing or feeling something. Self-regulation allows you to put yourself in another's shoes which allows for a positive emotional response as opposed to a careless reaction.

EQ Is Not for The Lazy.

Unmotivated individuals characteristically lack EQ. Motivation (and not just external, e.g. money, rewards, etc.) is what drives high EQ people. Personal goals, visions of success, a desire to make a difference, persistence and optimism are all examples of self-motivation.

Empathy is one of the most important and most valued elements of EQ. Not to be confused with sympathy or compassion, empathy is simply the understanding of another's emotions. This also ties into withholding judgement (self-regulation). Empathetic people understand when someone is feeling a certain way and respond accordingly to provoke a positive response.

Take a closer look at your feelings: If you are like most people these days then you are likely to find it difficult to sort your day from the hectic mess of appointments and deadlines that you must muddle through. As such, it can be difficult to correctly monitor your thoughts, much less your emotional state. This issue can then frequently be compounded even more by other stressors and distractions that can make it easy for poorly thought out actions to slip through which never do any good for anybody. Therefore, it is crucial that you get in the habit of practicing proper communication when you get a chance which means prioritizing communications with others when they do occur.

Emotions are often tied to events that take place in your immediate vicinity, but this doesn't automatically mean that they are valid. It is common for the emotion you are feeling right now, to be tied to something you have felt in the past that this situation is simply remining you of. If you find yourself dealing with this type of scenario, then regardless of how you feel in the moment, it is likely that you are dealing with an incorrect response which means you will need to work on limiting that association in your mind ASAP.

Learning to understand which emotions you are feeling now, and why, is a crucial step to improving your EQ in the long-term.

Being aware of your feelings is a skill which means that it can be improved if you are willing to practice doing so. To that end, you should pick a set time each day to practice this skill, once in the morning and then again in the evening. When practicing, you are going to want to check in with all of the emotions you have felt since your last check in and determine if the emotion you felt was an accurate response to the stimuli that was taking place at the time. Ideally, you are going to want to remember moments of intense emotion for the best effect.

Mindfulness
When it comes to habits that are easy to get started on, there are few that can do as much good, both physically and mentally, then mindfulness meditation. It has been an important part of the Buddhist faith for more than 2,00 years and has experienced a surge of popularity in the West over the past half a century for its ability to improve mental health, reduce stress, decrease anxiety and even aid in the recovery from drug addiction. Mindfulness meditation has been studied in earnest since the 1970s and the results have proven

so conclusive that it is even recommended as a common form of treatment for PTSD.

Mindfulness can also help to reduce pain and the reaction to pain. Some of the recent studies have suggested that unpleasant pain levels may be reduced up to 57% in beginner meditators. Studies have also shown that it can help the quality of life and mood of people that suffer from back pain and fibromyalgia, as well as chronic disorders like IBS, and in challenging illnesses like cancer and multiple sclerosis.

In addition, it can be physically shown to improve the rate at which information is processed and makes the brain all around healthier. It has also been shown to thicken the hippocampus which has the beneficial effect of making it easier for mindfulness meditation practitioners to learn and retain new information. This is in part also thanks to the fact that practicing mindfulness regularly creates additional folds in the cortex portion of the brain which goes hand in hand with an improved ability to make the right decision at the right moment.

Finally, it tends to cause the amygdala to be less active in regions responsible for stress, anxiety, and fear. With so many physical changes taking place in the brain, should it really come as a surprise that a survey of those who are in the habit of practicing mindfulness regularly found they were generally happier and more well-adjusted when compared to the populace as a whole?

The idea of practicing mindfulness first caught on in the Western world in the early part of the 1970s. Professor Jon Kabat-Zinn is credited with creating a mindfulness-based method of stress reduction which paired mindfulness with yoga to great result. While Zinn didn't do anything particularly new, the fact that his techniques led to measurable improvements for a wide variety of ailments both mental and physical in turn led to additional studies on the topic. These studies have shown time and again how effective practicing mindfulness can be which in turn has led to a steady increase in the practice to the point where it can now be found being regularly practiced in schools, veteran treatment facilities, hospitals, even prisons.

In addition to helping improve self-discipline, studies show that that taking 15 minutes out of your day to practice mindfulness meditation has a host of additional benefits as well. For starters, it is known to show dramatic increases when it comes to projecting a strong sense of self while at the same time noticeably reducing stress. This is thanks to the positive effects that mindfulness meditation has on attention span, emotional regulation and body awareness. What's even more impressive, neuroimaging has shown that mindfulness meditation allows those who practice it to process information more quickly than those who do not.

What's more, regularly practicing mindfulness is known to help with instances of meditators' minds getting stuck in negative thought patterns while also making it easier to focus for prolonged periods of time. A recent Johns Hopkins University study found that practicing mindfulness meditation regularly is equally effective at treating anxiety, depression, and ADHD as many commonly prescribed drugs.

While practicing mindfulness meditation might seem like a tall order at first, the truth of the matter is that being mindful is a habit which means you can learn to improve through practice, practice, practice. In fact, it should be one of the easier habits in this book to get accustomed to as it is as easy as taking a few moments out of your day to focus exclusively on the present via all the information that your senses are bringing in.

Getting Started with Mindfulness Meditation

While more fully connecting with every moment might sound like something that is beyond your ken, the fact of the matter is that once you commit the practice of mindfulness meditation to habit, the improved state will come to you quite quickly. What's more, once you understand the basics you will likely find that you can practice mindfulness meditation virtually anywhere if you can commit to being fully in the present and listening to the things your body is telling you.

While mindfulness meditation is exceedingly malleable, when you are first starting out you should set aside at least 15 minutes a day in a place that is free of distractions in order to start seeing benefits as quickly as possible. The space you choose should be somewhere you can feel truly relaxed and not have to worry about anything. As mindfulness meditation is all about getting in touch with yourself and the signals your body is sending you starting off with the fewest number of external stimuli is the preferable choice.

Form a routine: The easiest way to transition the act of mindfulness meditation into a habit is to start by making it part of your daily routine. As with any of the new habits discussed in these pages, letting your mind and body get used to the practice and expect it at the same time every day is crucial to keeping it around long enough for it to become a habit. As practicing mindfulness meditation requires nothing special and the benefits will not be immediately apparent, many people find it easy to make excuses to not practice regularly.

If you find that you are constantly coming up with excuses not to meditate then you will want to remember the ancient mindfulness saying which goes something like, "practice mindfulness meditation for 15 minutes per day; unless, of course, your schedule is very full in which case you will want to practice for 30 minutes." Don't use the outside world to make excuses that affect your potential for inner peace, find a few spare minutes each day and commit to doing so for 30 days, at the end of this time you will be glad you stuck with it.

Focus on the moment: While your end goal, while being mindful, should be to find a state of internal calm, regardless of what is going on in the world around you, it is difficult for most people to reach this state right away. Rather, they find it easier to start quieting their thoughts by focusing all their attention on the signals that their bodies are relaying to them in the moment.

While, at first, you may not feel as though you are processing too much data from the world around you, especially if you are practicing in a quiet, calm space as suggested, this could not be further from the truth. The fact of the matter is that most of the time your brain filters out around 80 percent of the information it receives on a given day which means that information is there, you just need to get in the habit of accessing it regularly.

Over time, you will learn to tune out the thoughts you have regarding your everyday routines and instead tap directly into whatever it is that is going on around you. When you do so, it is important to process the information that your senses are providing you, while at the same time making a conscious effort to not pass judgement or dig too deeply into anything that crosses your mind. Judging results in additional thoughts, one way or another, which tend to lead to even more thoughts, until it is practically impossible for you to focus on the task at hand.

Remember, when it comes to mindfulness meditation, the goal is to get as close as you can manage to the moment as possible, which means ignoring everything else that is going on, except for what your senses are providing you. To reach this state, you will start by focusing on your breathing, especially on the way the air feels as it enters and exits your lungs, along with the way it smells and tastes.

Make an effort to avoid judging what you feel: When you first begin practicing mindfulness meditation it is perfectly natural for your mind to intrude with thoughts about your current surroundings or to fill the void you are trying to achieve with a constant stream of consciousness. This occurs because over the years you have trained your brain to constantly be moving from one thought to the next in a rush to reach some conclusion or another.

When you find these errant thoughts breaching your sense of mental calm it is important to not interact with them as much as possible and instead to let them simply float away without interacting with them. If you find yourself getting sidetracked it is important to not attach a judgment to what has happened and to instead simply center yourself once more and continue as before. While this step is the most difficult for many people, it is important to keep it up until it becomes second nature as any interaction with the stray thoughts, even if it is just to chastise yourself for getting off track is an easy way to let even more thoughts through which will make it more difficult to find the state of mind that you are looking for.

Keep at it: When you first begin practicing mindfulness meditation it is important to do so with the right level of expectations regarding your results. Specifically, you will want to keep in mind that your mind is likely to wander frequently and that you will need to persevere through these periods if you are ever going to reach the level of mental quiet that you are looking for. To understand the ultimate mindset that you are striving for, you may find it helpful to consider the period of blankness the mind enters after a question has been asked but before the answer comes to you. Finding a way to reach this type of state is key to your long-term success.

Moving forward: Once you have started practicing being mindful regularly, you will find that the opportunity to do so will present itself practically everywhere you look. What follows are a few suggestions for finding mindfulness where you least expect it.

Be mindful when considering social media: While making a more concentrated attempt to single task will ultimately help you practice mindfulness more easily. Until you decide to do away with social media distractions, consider using them in a mindful manner instead. The next time you find yourself looking through old photographs, use that time to really remember the moment that each photograph was taken. Strain your memory and try and recall everything you can about the situation. What were the smells, the sounds, the sights? How did you feel in the moment? Really work to try and get back to that place to the extent that you block out external stimuli.

Practice mindfulness through dance: It doesn't matter who you are dancing with or why you are dancing in the first place, dancing itself is an inherently mindful act. Proper dancing requires the complete focus of the dancer both to ensure that the body follows as it should but also of the music, the tempo and the way they work together to affect the body. If you already love to dance, then all you need to do is be aware of the ways in which it helps you be mindful to take full advantage of their effects.

Make music mindfully: Much like dancing, playing music in such a way that it demands your attention is an inherently mindful action. If you take the time to focus on the moment and consider the way your body relates to the creation of each individual note. Consider the other musicians you are playing with and the ways the smallest change in what you are doing can affect the flow of the whole.

Do chores mindfully: While typically, household chores offer up little but daily drudgery, if you approach them with the idea that they can be a pathway to enlightenment you can help yourself see them in a whole new light. When it comes to practicing mindfulness in their midst, focus on each moment as it passes, take the time to clear your mind and let it be drawn to the way your hands feel while going through the motions. Make sure you focus on the smells, sights, and sounds and as you finish take a special moment to consider how much improved your space is now that it is clean.

Shower mindfully: Showering is another task that most people only complete on autopilot. Engage in the moment, practice mindfulness meditation as you go through the ritual of cleaning yourself. Shower time is typically a feast for the senses as there is something to occupy them all. Take the opportunity to really feel and notice these things and you will start or finish the day in a more mindful place.

Exercise mindfully: The brainwaves of those who are exercising are surprising like those who are meditating so it is only natural to combine the two for better results. This is an ideal time to focus on the senses as your body most likely has plenty to tell you while you are putting it through its paces. Take special care to focus on the smells and sights and how your body is responding to the stimuli all around you.

Conclusion

Just because you've finished this book doesn't mean there is nothing left to learn on the topic, and expanding your horizons is the only way to find the mastery you seek.

While it is certainly possible to start seeing results from the exercises described in the proceeding chapters right away, it is also possible that it will take you somewhat longer than that before any results begin to materialize. As such, if you start practicing a handful of exercises only to see few, if any, results right away, it is important to not get frustrated and throw in the towel on the whole CBT thing at once. Instead, it is important to stick with it and to try a variety of different exercises so you can get a better idea of what does, and does not, work for you. Remember finding success through CBT is a marathon, not a sprint, which means that slow and steady wins the race.

If you find this book helpful in anyway a review to support my endeavors is much appreciated.

Stephen Patterson

Cognitive Behavioral Therapy

www.ingramcontent.com/pod-product-compliance
Lightning Source LLC
Chambersburg PA
CBHW060454080526
44584CB00015B/1432